Beautiful Reflections

By:
Pepi

Cadmus Publishing
www.cadmuspublishing.com

Copyright © 2022 Pepi

Published by Cadmus Publishing
www.cadmuspublishing.com
Port Angeles, WA

ISBN: 978-1-63751-291-3

All rights reserved. Copyright under Berne Copyright Convention, Universal Copyright Convention, and Pan-American Copyright Convention. No part of this book may be reproduced, stored in a retrieval system, or transmitted in any form, or by any means, electronic, mechanical, photocopying, recording or otherwise, without prior permission of the author.

ACKNOWLEDGEMENTS

This beautiful struggle is dedicated to all of those who've helped me bear the burden of my difficult circumstances.

SPECIAL HONORS TO:
My loving mother **Ardella Mckenzie** (R.I.P.), Elizer Darris, Myon Burrell, Ambe Mckenzie, The All Square Team, Emily Hunter-Turner, John Geoppinger, Tish, Desdamonda, Malachi (Manifest) Kilgore, Jason Cheboya (R.I.P), Stillwater Poetry Group (SPG), Minnesota Prisoners Writers Workshop (MPWW), #MyonSpeaks, #UntilWeAreAllFree, #AllSquareMpls,Minnesotia's Poetry Community. Randall Smith (R.I.P.), Kevin Reese.

ABOUT THE AUTHOR

I am Mwati "Pepi" Mckenzie. I hail from Minneapolis, Minnesota. I was sentenced to life imprisonment twenty-eight years ago. Most would see incarceration as living a horrible existence. However, my resilience and brand perspective allowed me to view my sentence as a blessing. To be removed from mainstream society, and experience being in the presence of the so-called worst-of-the-worst is an experience most cannot survive or speak to.

However, I survived the madness, I overcame the debasement, the shame, the guilt, and the unethical rules that most who are incarcerated succumb to relegate themselves to a distinct class called, convicts. I retained the shards of my humanity and side-stepped the psychological destruction by doing the opposite of what convicts did; I utilized my time to formally educate myself. I utilized my time to reflect and ponder. I utilized my nonrenewable resource to write, in poetic form, my experiences. I hope this body of work inspires you to think deeper and reflect, ponder, improve, and overcome your circumstances – difficulties, failures, and use setbacks as blessings.

Pepi

Prologue

Beautiful reflections is what looked back at me as I stared at the world through cell bars.

Beautiful reflections is what looked back at me when I held my soul and judged myself.

These beautiful reflections mirror my beautiful struggle. A struggle that took thirty years of incarceration for me to compile, and reveal to mainstream society, without fear of being judged, ridiculed, or rejected.

These beautiful reflections will take you through my development and growth, my journey through introspection, luv and desirez, and my beautiful struggle.

This is not a work of fiction, these verses and stanzas are my "reality" – I hope you enjoy and allow these poetic verses to give you the energy and strength to look in your mirror, and use it as a tool to live in your reality without apologizing for who you are – Only U can judge U.

Pepi

Contents

Original Simplicity 3
False Optimisms or Wishful Thinking 5
Inner-Mind 6
Alone 7
Dark Clouds 8
The Looking Glass 9
Judgement Day 10
Burdens 11
Untitled 12
Natures Gift(s) 17
Amor 18
Eve's Flower 19
The Feminine U. 20
U 21
Black Luv- To: Niema 22
Divorce 23
Luv Ain't Supposed To Be This Hard 24
Luv Letter (Wyvonia) 25
Crazy Luv 27
Hypocrites 31
Hope 32
The Pain in My Face 33
A Nation Divided 34
America Eats its Children 35
Color-Blind 36
That Angel (Emily Hunter-Turner) 38
I Am My Hoodie 40

INTROSPECTION

PEPI

Original Simplicity

Oh original simplicity, strip away the
labyrinths of ignorance and delusions that
hinder me.

Rid that "I" in me that hinders me
from being who I am and not who I
appear to be.

Wake me from these night terrors, I want
to hug reality,
Let the Holiness understand my sin,
Let my Greater embrace my lesser,
Let my pain caress my joy.

I tried suicide, it wouldn't allow me to die
to myself – my ego followed me to the next
realm and illuminated my misdemeanor
thoughts and desires.

That iron grip of ignorance interferes with
the internal infinite ocean, I call my divine-
self.

Oh original simplicity, help me unfold from
within. Let my chaotic anger, crude opinions,
secret lusts, and harmful folly dissipate
like morning dew as it harmonizes with the
afternoon sun.

Aid me in curing the diseases that prevent
me from enjoying my reflection, clinging to
purity, and adhering to self abnegation.

Let me stand against me in judgement and
be the witness to my inner turmoil –
strip my flesh away to reveal the hollowness
inside that exhibits righteousness, patience
and compassion.

Oh original simplicity, help me slay my
illusions and fill my chalice with perfect
reality – I yearn to know if I am my

sins.

False Optimisms or Wishful Thinking

Where I'm from you either Crippin, Folks,
Bloods, or Lords, so we don't cross the
line.

We use those lines to destroy the days
of our beautiful lives.
We crush hopes and kill lucid dreams.
We raise our children to believe what we
believe, so they invest in evil deeds –
This wishful thinking and false optimism
we title: "keepin it real."

The psychosis stems from that tart generational
breast milk. Now, we live in warzones
and six by nine enclosures.

How do we repair the harm?
How do we accept the grief and loss?
How do we reverse the excruciating pain?

I say we blame the color of our skin
and neglect the reality that it's the
mentality we live in.

Inner-Mind

Amenta is a land of strange happenings.
Like the turmoil of a passing nightmare,
Where the adversity is individualistic, like the silent power of truth.

ALONE

Turmoil, suffering, pain.
Where man hates to go,
Everlasting purgatory,
To many, loneliness is a dreadful place.

Dark Clouds

Eyez closed so I can see the darkness
that lies within my soul.
The luv I thought I deserved wasn't
enough because it lacked growth.

Seeking internal peace, so I look in
the bottom of a bottle or another
substance to help me cope.

In retrospect, I lived my life from
corner-to-corner and street-to-street,
you know, that block life. As a result
of the drama and trauma I lost hope.

I wish I was a sheep then the Lord
could guide me. Since my life is steeped
in sin, I only know oppression, dark
clouds, depression, people telling me
to make peace with my past, and reach
for hope.

Truth be told, making peace with my
past allows me to slow down and
seek a positive energy.

Denying the luv I think I
deserve will help me grow.

Them blocks and corners are a thing
of the past – finally, I can open my
eyez and enjoy the essence of my soul.

THE LOOKING GLASS

Reflected appraisals.

Internalization and Acts from a social perspective.

An alter-ego that shapes boundaries.

Socializing agents that circumscribe my dreams – I am who I am supposed to be because of my socio-economic class.

The looking glass is too small to see my soul, so I wallow in purgatory until my soul whispers in my ear.

From an infant to getting too old to be shaped like clay – Married and relinquishing my rib, to looking into the mirror and seeing my spirit decay from a co-opted perspective.

Woe! to the reflected appraisals who grasp my essence.

Judgement Day

I stand before you black as coal, so deep within me, there's a diamond I call it my soul.

I need guidance to rid myself of the ills that plague my tormented psyche. I want to caress that bloody shadow that crept into my dreams.

I climbed the heights to Maccu Picchu's citadel to cling to your majestic essence, only to come away with dew and the bloody feather from a condor.

I dug deep into the bowels of the earth, only to find soil black like me, boulders heavy like my burdens, and glistening oil that seeped through my battered hands.

To and fro I searched. From the highest heights to the deepest depths, in between, that flickering mirror I failed to look in.

I prayed on my knees until they were bruised. I prayed until my knuckles bled; I wanted to quit but the Glock misfired. I shaped each puzzle piece and couldn't solve the riddle of my inner turmoil or my forbidden desires.

I read about the caves the prophets meditated in. Attended the churches, mosques, and synagogues too many tormented souls prayed for forgiveness in, In between, that flickering mirror waited for me to judge me.

BURDENS

I'll forever be pinned to the cross.
This burden of mine is too much.
I luv her but she says it's not enough.
Where do I go from here? Every step
is not enough.

If I act out, they'll say I'm doing too much.
If I lay back, they'll say I'm not doing enough.
If I speak up, they'll say I should shut my
mouth.
Sometimes I feel like there's no way out
I'm trapped pulling the nails out of my
palms to alleviate the pain.

No screams, tearz or shouts.
Burdens from the past like the
African holocaust.
Classism and my dark pigment keeps me
trapped,
My color is seeped in pain,
These revelations are burdens like Christ
on a cross,
My revelations blind Christians so they
stay lost.
I'm a felon looking to fit in mainstream
society, who's the boss?

Black like a stallion running to avoid the
cross,
friends is enemies, I stay away to avoid
the double-cross.

Untitled

I trade poker faces with my reflection;
it's traumatic like doing burpies on a bed of
nails,

Expressing myself with a quil-pen dipped in
blood – A story that is torrid, what a
painful tale.

I've been given the ingredients to destroy
my soul in an earthen container, so I
cook up drama and let the story be told.

The things that manifests itself through
my struggle I call a Ghetto Rose. That
catacomb of carnal pleasure is painful.
Yet, I refuse to seek assistance – The
depression and low self esteem doesn't
divert the painful things that surge
through me, my hearts too cold.

My mind is full of demons,
This tight face and black heart only limits
my choices to a pine box, cell block, or
something more painful like art by Basquiat.

BEAUTIFUL REFLECTIONS

PEPI

LUV AND DESIREZ

PEPI

NATURES GIFT(S)

Compositions of life.
River ways, creeks that bend, waters that fall.
I touched the grass,
I saw the firmament,
Metew Neter speaks in different tints.

Amor

I saw her fullness the other night.
Like the mythological goddess Hathor – the amorous Queen,
she guided me with her light.

Eve's Flower

The organic love of Isis' flower,
Petals of velvet satin,
Seductive thoughts – Bliss,
Touches from the mystery of passions celestial waters,
The art of Nephthys's enchantment,
Behold, the flowers in the Garden of Hetep.

The Feminine U.

If I could walk through her beautiful mind, I would:
Gently caress her desires.
Boldly yield to her self-restraint.
Whisper to her feelings and console her anxieties.
Give homage to her values.
Like, Afini, Assatta, and Ida B. Wells, I'd admire the warrior spirit in her.
Protect the keys to her feminine secrets and dance to her rhythm.

Taste the sweet nectar of the rose that blossoms in her psyche.
Cloak myself in her imagination.
Batter and bruise the doubts, fears, and domestic woes.
Like a black knight, protect her essence and resilient spirit from the foes that disregard her dignity.
Bow to her needs, wants, and aspirations.

Faithfully, support and understand her struggle.
Enjoy her felicity and harmony.
I'd say wow to her style; I like how she modulates.
Massage the thoughts of a long day.
When I exit her beautiful mind, I'll tell her in Swahili, I value the feminine U.

U

U remind me of Atlanta, sweet peaches hanging from a tree,

I saw U in New Orleans, a magnolia, pretty like that white, yellow, purple rose sprouting in spring,

U resemble Minnesota, ten thousand lakes that are beautiful in Autumn,

When U appear my heart beats like a drum,

Ur smile is overpowering like rum,

I'm speechless, U smile, I am numb,

U acknowledge my presence, with pride and joy, I am overcome.

BLACK LUV- TO: NIEMA

It's deeper than the bowels of earth or
a mathematicians equations,

It's never a touch of lust,

It's a combination of comfort and respect,

The psyche that produces rose petals at your feet,

Like liaisons, our spirits are mutually blended –
That's the mystery unseen,

Souls moving in unison is the hug we gave
each other last week,

The warmth of brilliance and resilience has
no boundaries, so we build,

The primary substance that binds is respect
and admiration,

Dedication is the weapon on the battlefield
of doubt; what is this ecology?

BLACK LUV.

DIVORCE

You say you love me but you can't look
me in the eye,

You lay down beside me, wake up in the
morning telling lies.

In 2 deep who'd ever think love between
the sheets was akin to poison ivy.

The I do turned into an I don't,
we don't see eye-to-eye
That walk down the aisle turned into a
goodbye,
That love turned into an I won't
That love turns into a cry, now I'm wondering
why.

The pain of a wedding ring,
The gleam of the diamonds are my pain,
The veil shrouds her eyes that cry,
I tried to apologize, I guess it's over
when a dove cries.

When life ills and past traumas are a wedge,
the love is gone,
The wedding photos are a glimpse of better dayz-
Sorry for the pain, but what's life without rain.

Luv Ain't Supposed To Be This Hard

Smiles and frowns,
Ups and downs.
Used to be a happy home, it's broken now,
She use to love being around, she strays now.
I saw her crooked smile when I gave her
those jewels.

Luv ain't supposed to be this hard.

It went from exchanging wedding rings,
Answering the phone on the first ring,
I miss you and kisses.
Now she ignores my calls and does her own
thing. I see the deceit dripping from her
wedding ring; what's a man to do?

Luv ain't supposed to be this hard.

I remember, we met and hit it off,
strawberries, champagne, and roses.
Sweethearts day is the coldest,
That love turned into a cold shoulder,
She don't love me like she says she do.

Luv ain't supposed to be this hard.

Staring in the mirror, I had to confess,
ain't no love left,
The last time she saw me, she rolled her
eyes,
The last time I saw her it was love in
disguise, although we said I do, I'm looking
at the pain through my rearview – That shoulder
is too cold, so I'm looking for a love that's
new.

Luv Letter (Wyvonia)

I'm honkin and beep beepin. Ride with me or
let's walk around the lake and hold hands.
Matter of fact, let's walk on the beach with
our toes immersed in the black sand,
If you want, we can listen to a soulful band.

Here's a letter, check the box if we go together.
I make a heart with the shape of my hand when
we're not together,
Luv letters to you even in stormy weather,
Don't take this luv for granted, we look good
together.

On those sunny days, I just smile and stare into
your eyez.
You and that sexy smile,
we cuddle from sunset until a moonrise.

You get mad cuz I play too much, yet, we still
together like spy versus spy.
Our names are carved in an oak tree, in between,
is a plus sign.
Chocolates in the mail – special delivery. It's
Sweethearts Day cuz the candy goes good with
your thighs.

We accept each others faults, mishappenings, and secrets.
When we conversate, unlike others, we go the deepest,
Like sugar in my coffee. You are the sweetest,
You are that Queen, the prettiest.

When I have whip cream dreams you paint the scene,
Dear Wyvonia: This letter is for you because you're not an option, you are the other half of me.

CRAZY LUV

My finger tips caress your skin, my tongue follows
your curves while our synergy comingle,

Diving in your mind after a late night searching
for clues to define what that was,

Last night was the wildest, can we do that
again, as crazy as it was.

Passion, more sweat, followed by more passion,
water to recover from dehydration, crazy luv;
damn, that's what that was?

There is no amount of scents, roses, or candy that
can replace that space – Remember the smell,
the touch, the taste, as crazy as it was?

PEPI

BEAUTIFUL STRUGGLE

PEPI

HYPOCRITES

U make laws and use them against those Black like me. I call it hypocrisy.

Criminalize my existence and erect fences, walls, and call them projects and ghettos.

U create fears from my image and tell the world you're just tryin to civilize me with them laws U use against those who like me.

Equality and justice is free powdered milk and cheese. I'm excluded from education, occupations, and occupancy; justice ain't equal, why does the law lie to me?

Society turns a blind-eye and wonders why the pain is reflected in the flames, can't you see the flames illuminate the hypocrisy.

What is a hypocrite to integrity? It's similar to protesters, rubber bullets, and riot police, they don't go together.

Public policy and city streets, the pain is real but the system doesn't feel – It's worse than black backs bent picking cotton in a field.

Hope

The Attorney General and the President, in the name of hope, sold guns to the Mexican cartel,

North America's elected predecessors increased locking people in cells,

Too many ex-cons facing the feds for possession and gun sales,

It's more guns than people; The Second Amendment is expressing itself,

The NRA sets the stage,

Politicians accept the payment and spit the spin,

Who buys into the agenda?

Dissidents pay their part – the rest of society are the thespians, who cat as if they don't know,

Meanwhile, in the public housing sector, their strapped and ready to go,

Immoral decadence embedded in the Declaration of Independence,

Homeland security watches the border while Wall Street gets a cut from every gun sold,

The lead and copper smelted represents a ticker symbol that coincides with an IPO,

American opulence comes with a clip, bullets, and a scope no matter the community, no matter the school, no matter the church, no matter how much hope.

The Pain in My Face

The pain in my face. – the angst,

The homicides in my state,

The exorbitant incarceration rates that take place,

The double bunks without enough space,

The prison industries that commit economic rape,

The Brother's with kids they can't raise,

Are the Black angels on the way?

Is the Most-High aware of the spiritual decay? If not, I need to pray for a better way.

Parolee's and the jobless rates equal a duffle bag, a felony point and an interstate leading the way,

The pain my face mirros the things that are not adjacent to a healthy mental state,

The pain in my face can't smile until this journey leads to a better place.

A Nation Divided

Meritocracy equals black folk making it
if they try hard and not factor in classism
European Patriarchal systems that rely
on stereotypes, and institutionalized racism,

Political, cultural, socioeconomic violence creates
obstacles.
With a little hope and a prayer to white
Jesus, the semi-exculpatory clauses may
help you overlook the Original Sin and
the imperialistic doctrine,

Patriotism divides black bodies from the
American agenda – Red, white, blue are
the sadistic experiments conducted by
Thomas Jefferson on Slaves.

The Constitution is shrouded in J.
Marion Sims gynecological celebrations
and the pursuit of Happiness' lowered
expectations.

Urban renewal and gentrification are one-
and-the same.

We are divided by corporate-dominated
politics, two-party collusion and National
predators we call the 12 monkeys who
are guarded by sins of omission and
bureaucratic incompetence.

AMERICA EATS ITS CHILDREN

Gazin at the shores from the Mayflower;
ain't that America?

Ain't that America's children, the remnants
from the Nina, Pinta, Santa Maria, and
Jesus' Transatlantic Voyage, imperialism
and Columbus's love child?

Ain't that America, Home of the Slave's,
Land of the Colonist's, it's social classes
with its warsaw-like Black ghettos,
Reservations, Concentration camps, and
Barrio's?

Ain't that America, the powers that be,
praying to jingoism, xenophobia, and
parochial dogmatic religions?

Ain't that America with its legalized
pharmaceuticals: despair, agony, hate, rage,
and lethargism?

Ain't that America and its Republicans,
Democrats, Capitalists, Socialists, Communists
with their draconian welfare nanny
propagandistic patriotic benevolence programs,
that the Nazi's adopted to become socially
acceptable?

Fratricide! Genocide! Outright murder
of the Peoples values, moral system,
virtuistic endeavors, benevolent ecosystem
and Pursuits of Happiness – Gazing at
the shores, Ain't that America eating
its children?

Color-Blind

I am color-blind because inequality does
not exist.

I am color-blind because Jim Crow and the
Black Codes are not refined and incarcerates
enmass.

I am color-blind because the Tea Party
doesn't want reconstruction or big government,
they just want their country back.

I am color-blind because right-wing extremists
don't subscribe to Lee Atwater's racial
subtexts and buzzwords.

I am color-blind because low taxes equates
to 1957's conservative golden age with no
civil rights.

I am color-blind because the Brady Bill
is titled Brady and the Affordable Health
Care Act is a besmirch called Obama
Care.

I am color-blind because I don't see
police brutality as an extension of the
oppressors agenda.

I am color-blind because I don't see
that Hernando Cortes Committed an act
of genocide in Tenochtitlan.

I am color-blind because I don't see that
the Native Americans lands were illegally
seized and appropriated.

I am color-blind because sexism, classism,
pogromism, oppression, poverty, racism are
not psychological, theological,
legislative, educational, ethnic, economical,
cultural, political, occupational, and
institutionalized warfare.

I am color-blind, I am color-blind, I
am color . . .

#UntilWeAreAllFree

That Angel (Emily Hunter-Turner)

The way I see it, ain't no equal fight.
Different day different struggle,
Every day every night, observing the sky for
that Angel,

Who can bring compassion to the struggle?
Who can soften my heart and restore faith?
Why is it that I am praying with clenched
fists seeking deliverance?

Who will wipe the blood from my eyez?
Who can relieve that mental anguish experienced
from those dark alleys called County Jails
and Courtrooms?
Where is that compassion for the rolling stones
and flowers that abandoned their wombs?

Who will hug our enemies we call addictions?
Who will cherish a young life that is abandoned
too soon?
Where is that Angel to pave the way?
Who is it that will help me return to the
slums to bring light and life for those seeking
a better way?

I need a miracle to repair broken homes,
Where is the solution to the homelessness
we call pain?
Who will give deference to the disfranchised
and ashamed?

That Angel wiped my tears away so I
can give voice to the chaotic noise, now
I'm in the middle of her perfect storm,
that Angel is evidence of a Divine Presence,
so we can tear down these traps and
protect the communities essence.

#AllSquareMpls

I Am My Hoodie

If I'm my Hoodie where can I go?
His family buried their first born because
of his Hoodie,
Can I wear it in a boardroom,
what about a court room?

Should I put it on when I see Ol' boy who
told,
Maybe it's just for the poor and disfranchised
can I wear it to a disfranchised vote,

What Hood should I say I'm from,
What block,
What corner,
What Alley,
What fold,

What if I look like Trayvon, will I make it
home,
What if my Hoodie the wrong size,
I guess the answer to those questions
is my Hoodie dictates where I go,
If I have Potential to grow or who I know –
textiles are intricately linked to our destiny.

When you wear your Hoodie don't drive
with the hood on, that's the reason they
pull you over for,
your hands are up and your Hoodie ain't
bullet proof, that's the reason they shoot
you for.

Pretexts, prejudices, and racialized outcomes,
they have hoods on in the Courtrooms.
Knees on our backs and necks,
Choke-hold and disrespect – my Hoodies
hasn't stopped it yet?

In penetentary's, joints, and prisons Hoodies
are forbidden,
we are depersonalized, spiritually vandalized,
dehumanized and doused with psychological
bluez, - Can my Hoodie stop that?

Tookie was executed because he tried
to save the kids; his Hoodie was a paper
and pen.
Does your Hoodie take a stand?
Does a slogan make you a man?
Does a slogan make a black life matter?
A Glock tucked away in your Hoodie,
I wonder how that will end.

#IAmMyHoodie
#JasonCole
#MyonSpeaks

PEPI

www.ingramcontent.com/pod-product-compliance
Lightning Source LLC
Chambersburg PA
CBHW071917070526
44583CB00016B/2024